ANIMALS
BY THE
NUMBERS

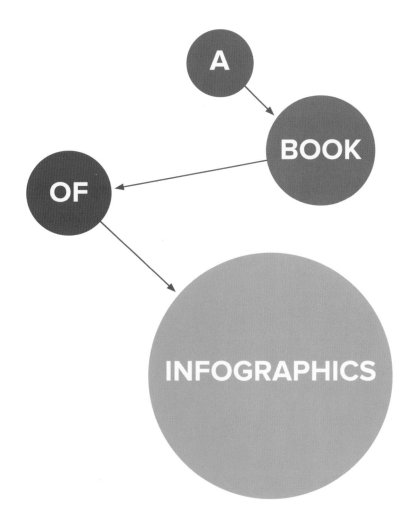

A → BOOK → OF → INFOGRAPHICS

STEVE JENKINS

HOUGHTON MIFFLIN HARCOURT · BOSTON · NEW YORK

In this book
The graph shows how many times different kinds of animals appear in this book.

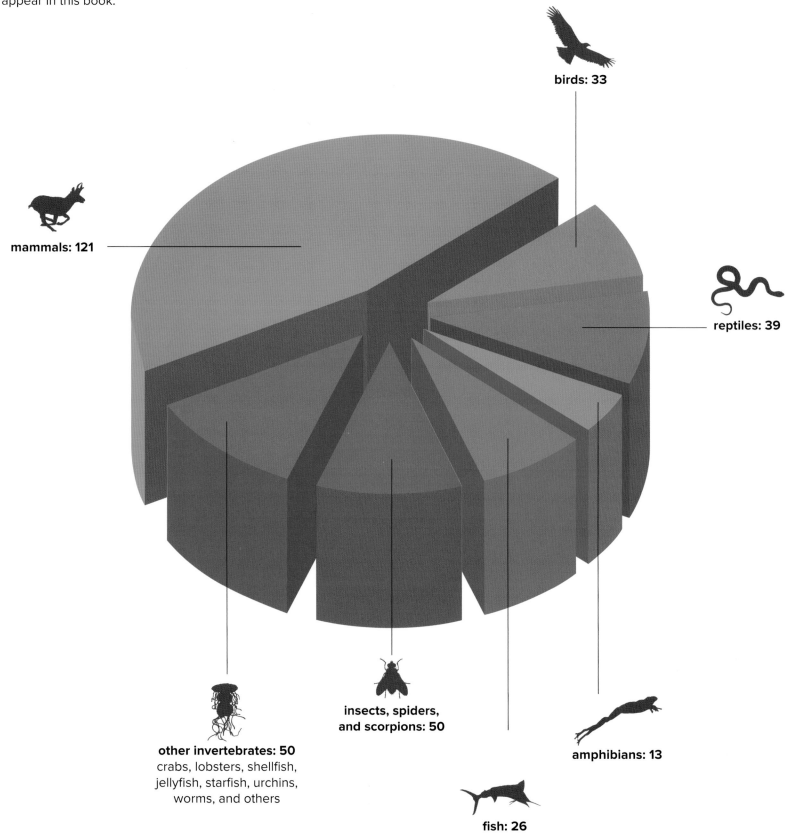

birds: 33

reptiles: 39

mammals: 121

other invertebrates: 50
crabs, lobsters, shellfish, jellyfish, starfish, urchins, worms, and others

insects, spiders, and scorpions: 50

amphibians: 13

fish: 26

Numbers help us understand our world. We use numbers to measure and compare things. Numbers help us explain what happened in the past and predict what might happen in the future.

When it comes to animals, numbers are especially important. How big is a whale? How fast is a cheetah? How loud is a lion's roar? It would be difficult to answer these questions—even to ask them—without numbers.

In this book, facts and figures about animals are presented visually as graphs, symbols, and illustrations. These infographics give us another way of looking at animals and understanding some of the amazing things that they can do.

CONTENTS

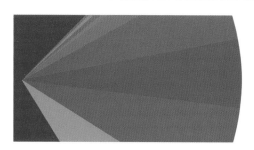

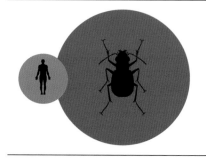

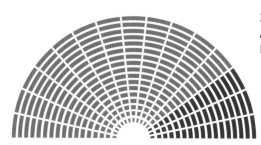

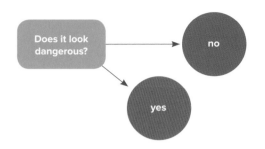

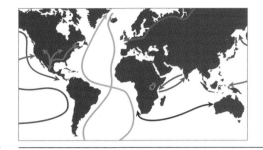

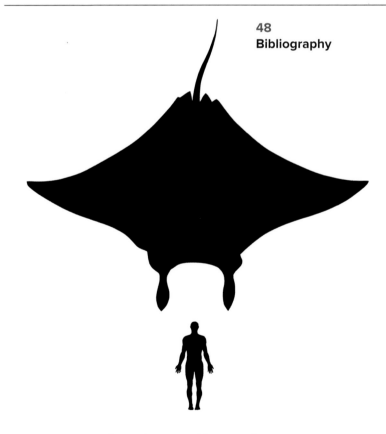

A manta ray and human shown
at the same scale.

Fur, feathers, skin, and scales

Scientists often divide the animal world into two groups: creatures with and without backbones.

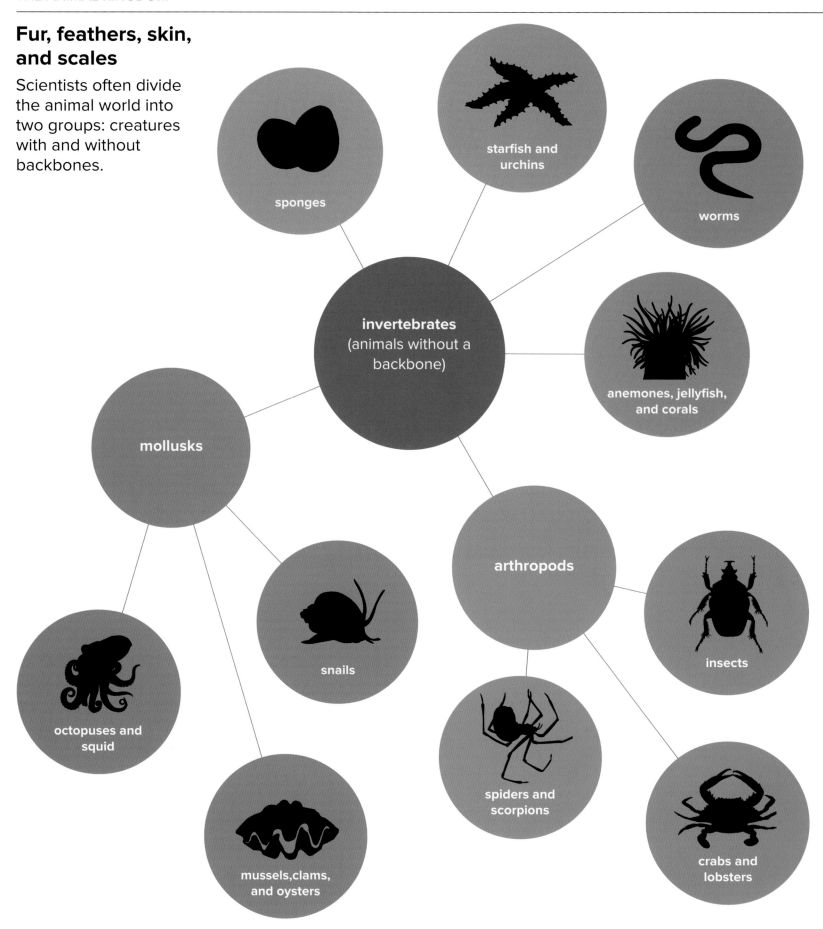

sponges

starfish and urchins

worms

invertebrates (animals without a backbone)

anemones, jellyfish, and corals

mollusks

arthropods

octopuses and squid

snails

insects

spiders and scorpions

crabs and lobsters

mussels, clams, and oysters

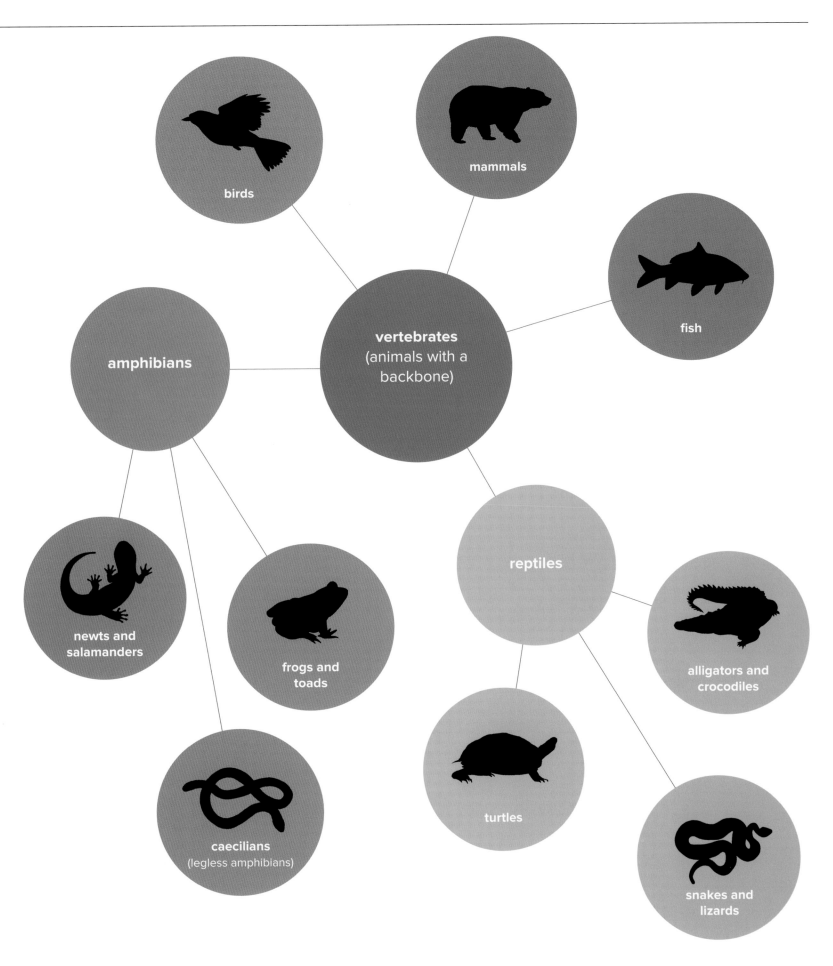

birds

mammals

fish

amphibians

vertebrates
(animals with a
backbone)

newts and
salamanders

frogs and
toads

reptiles

alligators and
crocodiles

caecilians
(legless amphibians)

turtles

snakes and
lizards

Millions of animals

So far, well over a million species of animals have been named. Thousands of new species are discovered every year, and there are probably millions more yet to be found.

What is a species?
The basic unit that biologists use to organize the animal kingdom is the *species*. Members of a species usually look and act alike, and can mate and produce offspring.

amphibians
7,450
species

reptiles
10,000
species

birds
10,400
species

fish
32,900
species

crustaceans
67,000
species

other invertebrates
(animals without backbones)
72,000
species

mollusks
90,000
species

spiders and scorpions
102,000
species

Most animals are insects, and the largest group of insects is the beetles. Of all the animals known to science, more than one in four is a beetle.

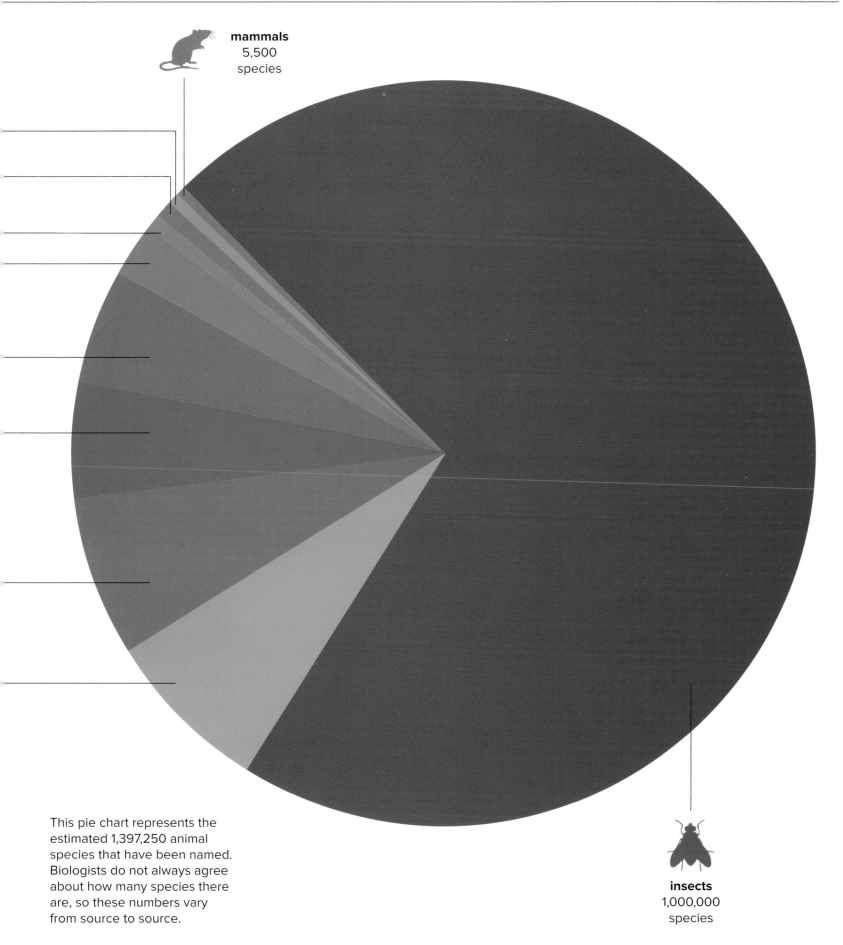

mammals
5,500
species

This pie chart represents the estimated 1,397,250 animal species that have been named. Biologists do not always agree about how many species there are, so these numbers vary from source to source.

insects
1,000,000
species

Little & big

Some of the smallest and largest animals of the past and present.

The **Mososaur,** a terrifying ocean predator, died out with dinosaurs 66 million years ago. The tiny **Amau frog** was discovered only recently.

 animals alive today

 extinct animals

Giants

These animals are shown at the same scale as the human figure.

1 *Megalodon* (extinct 2½ million years ago)

2 **whale shark**

3 **grizzly bear**

4 **African elephant**

5 **Moa** (extinct 1400 A.D.)

6 **oarfish**

7 *Argentinosaurus* (extinct 90 million years ago)

8 **hippopotamus**

9 **ground sloth** (extinct 6,250 years ago)

10 **blue whale**

11 **Titanboa** (extinct 58 million years ago)

12 **reticulated python**

13 **colossal squid**

14 **manta ray**

15 *Quetzalcoatlus* (extinct 66 million years ago)

16 *Mososaurus* (extinct 66 million years ago)

17 **saltwater crocodile**

18 *Sarcosuchus* (extinct 208 million years ago)

19 *Indricotherium* (extinct 23 million years ago)

20 *Tyrannoaurus rex* (extinct 66 million years ago)

Life size

These animals—some of the smallest of their kind—are shown at actual size.

1 bee hummingbird
2 dwarf goby
3 Amau frog
4 pygmy seahorse
5 *Brookseia* chameleon
6 *Wolfi* octopus
7 thread snake
8 bumblebee bat

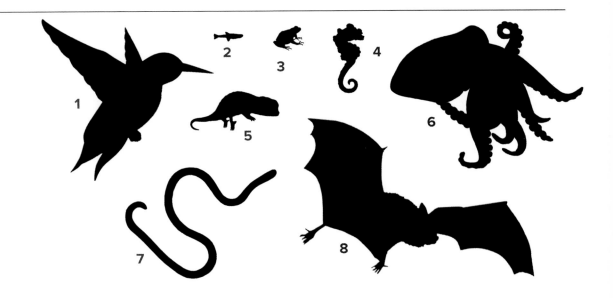

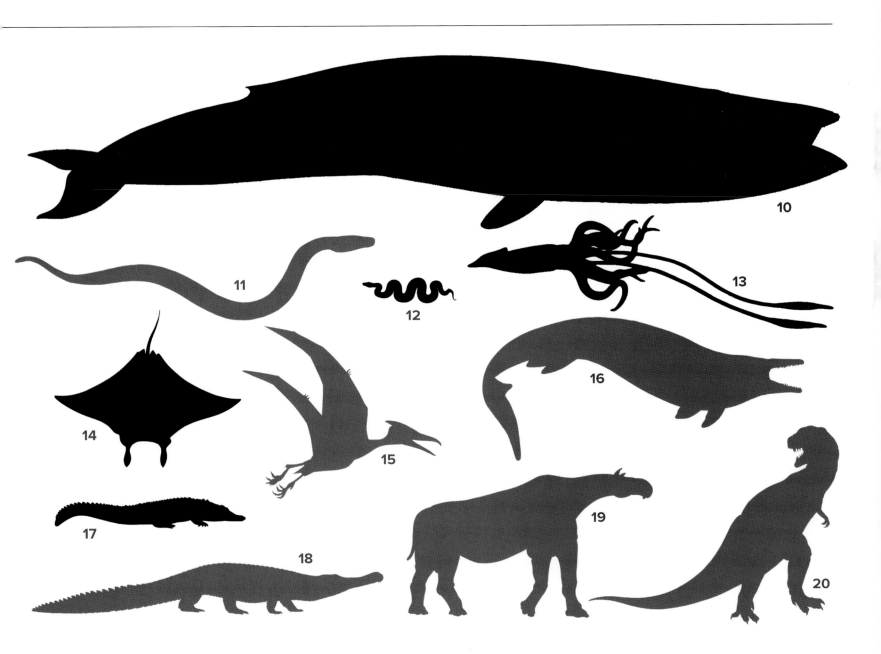

How much do all the humans on earth weigh?

If we could add up the weight of every person on earth, the result would be the biomass of the world's humans. This isn't practical, so human biomass—350 million tons—is just an estimate. It's impossible to accurately count the world's insects or fish, so the figures given for their biomass are based on what scientists have learned about an animal's population and average weight.

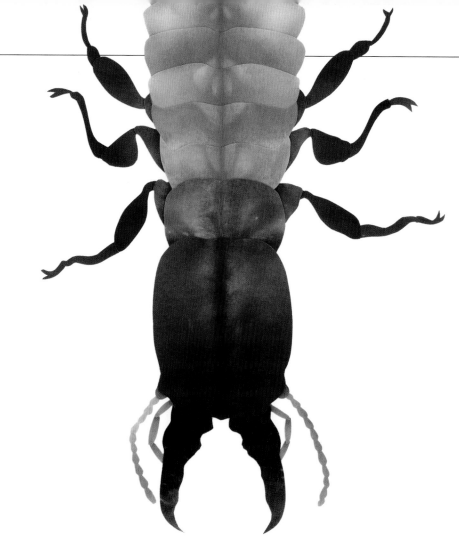

Most people have never seen a **bristlemouth,** a small deep-sea fish. But some scientists think that bristlemouths and **termites** might outweigh every other kind of animal. Creatures like these are impossible to count accurately, so estimates of their biomass vary widely.

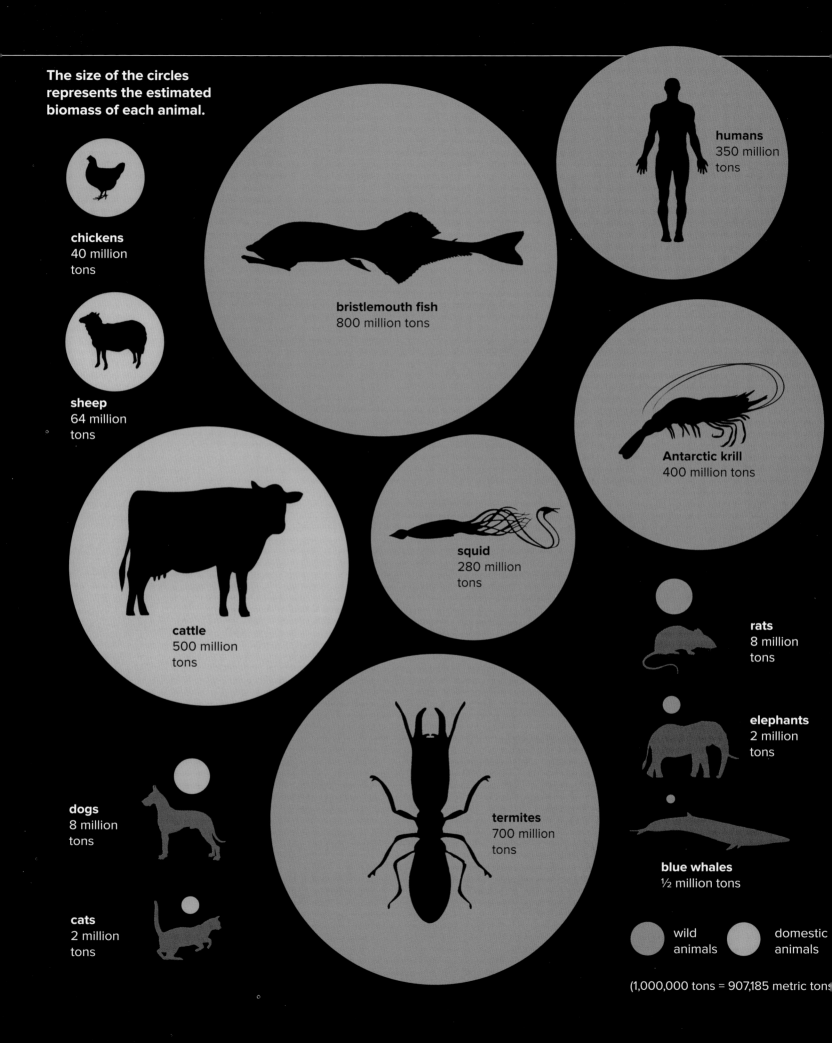

The size of the circles represents the estimated biomass of each animal.

chickens
40 million tons

sheep
64 million tons

bristlemouth fish
800 million tons

humans
350 million tons

Antarctic krill
400 million tons

cattle
500 million tons

squid
280 million tons

rats
8 million tons

elephants
2 million tons

dogs
8 million tons

termites
700 million tons

blue whales
½ million tons

cats
2 million tons

wild animals

domestic animals

(1,000,000 tons = 907,185 metric tons)

And the heavyweight champion is . . .

It is estimated that all the insects on earth weigh almost 300 times as much as all the humans. There may be more than 15 tons (13,600 kilograms) of insects for every person on earth.

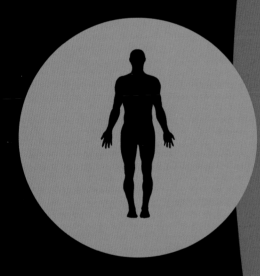

humans
350 million tons

all insects
100 billion tons

How fast?

Many animals survive by being swift fliers, runners, or swimmers. Animals use their speed to catch prey or to avoid becoming prey themselves.

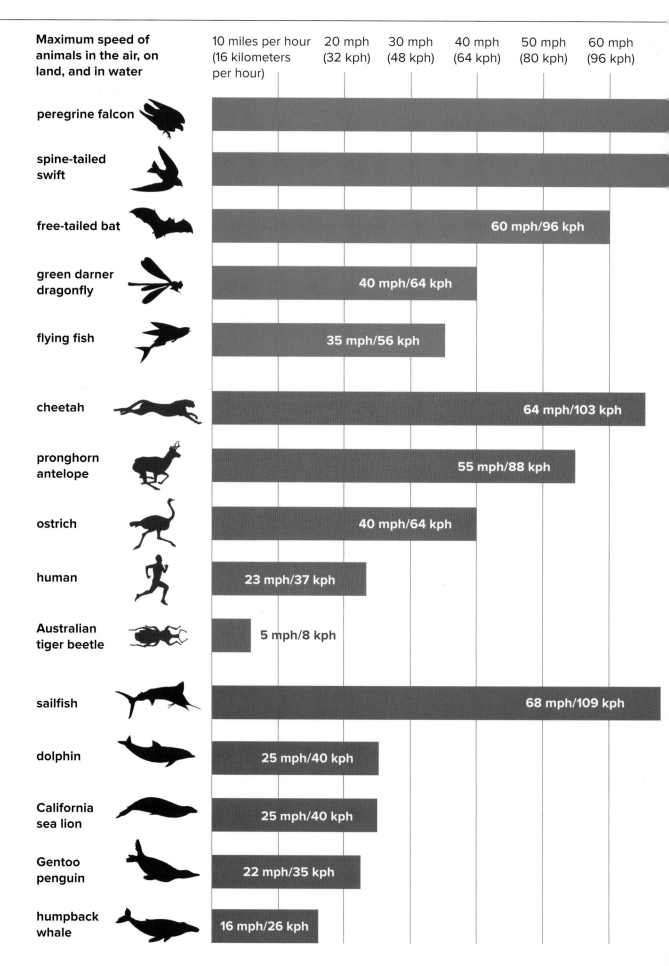

Maximum speed of animals in the air, on land, and in water

	10 miles per hour (16 kilometers per hour)	20 mph (32 kph)	30 mph (48 kph)	40 mph (64 kph)	50 mph (80 kph)	60 mph (96 kph)

peregrine falcon

spine-tailed swift

free-tailed bat — 60 mph/96 kph

green darner dragonfly — 40 mph/64 kph

flying fish — 35 mph/56 kph

cheetah — 64 mph/103 kph

pronghorn antelope — 55 mph/88 kph

ostrich — 40 mph/64 kph

human — 23 mph/37 kph

Australian tiger beetle — 5 mph/8 kph

sailfish — 68 mph/109 kph

dolphin — 25 mph/40 kph

California sea lion — 25 mph/40 kph

Gentoo penguin — 22 mph/35 kph

humpback whale — 16 mph/26 kph

speed in air

speed on land

speed in water

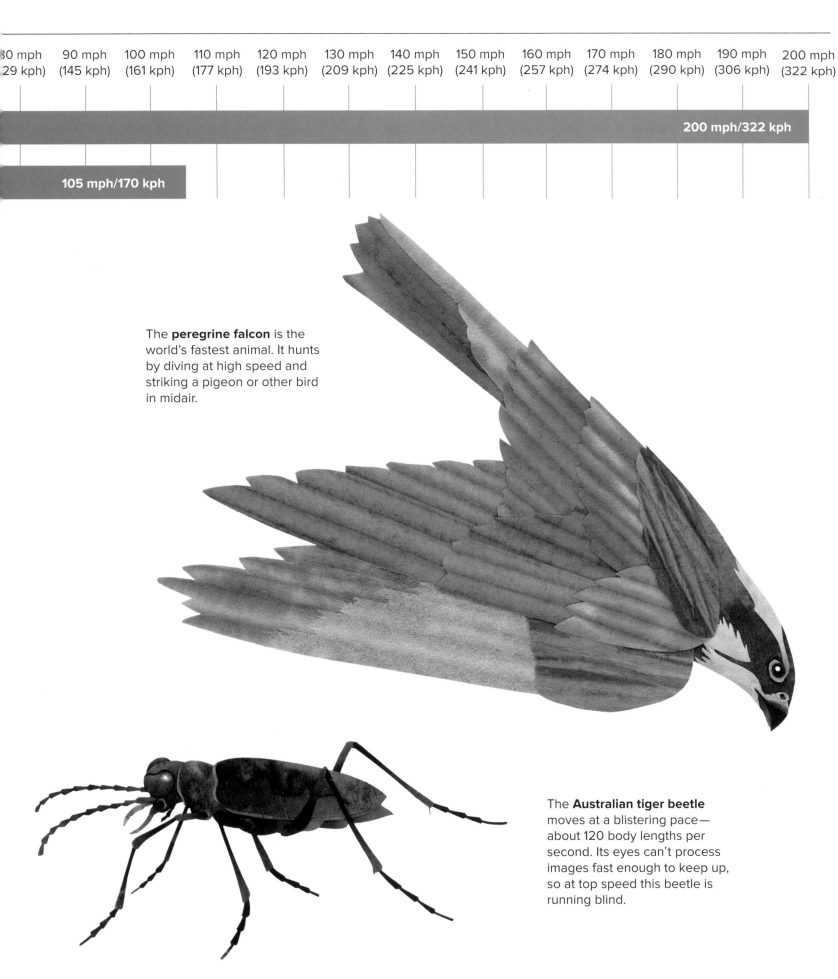

80 mph
(129 kph)

90 mph
(145 kph)

100 mph
(161 kph)

110 mph
(177 kph)

120 mph
(193 kph)

130 mph
(209 kph)

140 mph
(225 kph)

150 mph
(241 kph)

160 mph
(257 kph)

170 mph
(274 kph)

180 mph
(290 kph)

190 mph
(306 kph)

200 mph
(322 kph)

200 mph/322 kph

105 mph/170 kph

The **peregrine falcon** is the world's fastest animal. It hunts by diving at high speed and striking a pigeon or other bird in midair.

The **Australian tiger beetle** moves at a blistering pace— about 120 body lengths per second. Its eyes can't process images fast enough to keep up, so at top speed this beetle is running blind.

Jump!

Some animals hunt by lying in wait, then pouncing on their prey. Others use their leaping ability to get to safety when a predator attacks.

Leaping distance and leaping distance compared to body length

 distance jumped in feet/meters

 distance jumped times body length

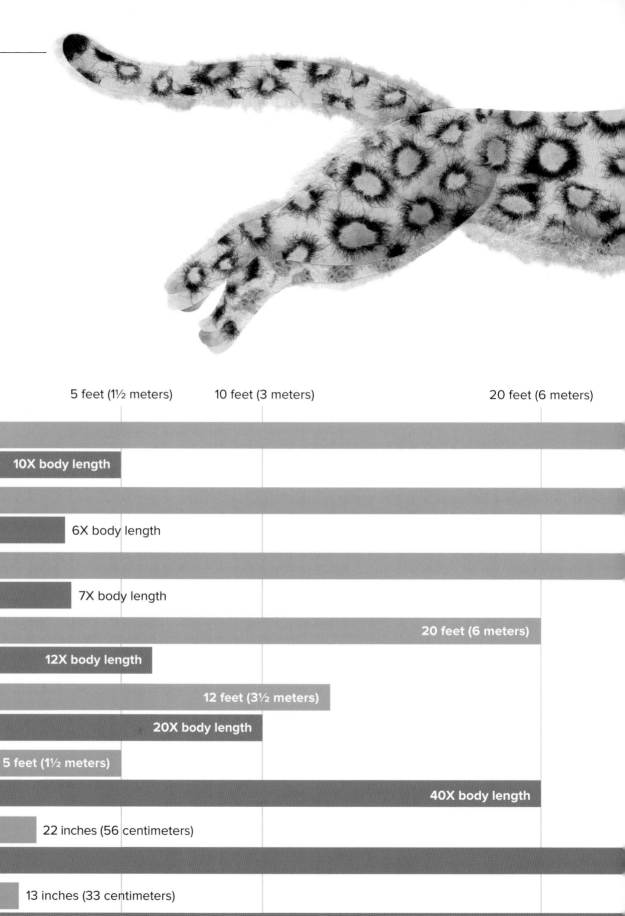

	5 feet (1½ meters)	10 feet (3 meters)	20 feet (6 meters)

snow leopard

10X body length

red kangaroo

6X body length

impala

7X body length

jackrabbit

20 feet (6 meters)

12X body length

kangaroo rat

12 feet (3½ meters)

20X body length

southern cricket frog

5 feet (1½ meters)

40X body length

froghopper

22 inches (56 centimeters)

flea

13 inches (33 centimeters)

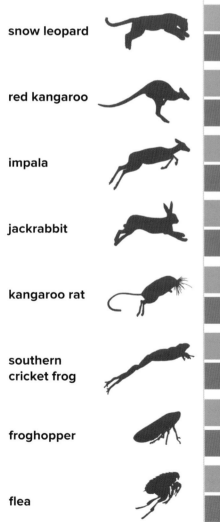

	10X body length	20X body length	40X body length

A **snow leopard** can jump 50 feet (15 meters), farther than any other land animal. But the **froghopper** may be the animal leaping champion, leaping 112 times its body length. If the snow leopard could match this insect's performance, it could jump the length of two football fields.

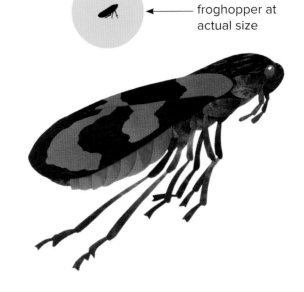

froghopper at actual size

30 feet (9 meters)   40 feet (12 meters)   50 feet (15 meters)

50 feet (15 meters)

30 feet (9 meters)

33 feet (10 meters)

112X body length

100X body length

60X body length   80X body length   100X body length

Flap faster!

An animal must beat its wings to fly. Usually, the smaller an animal, the faster it has to flap its wings to stay airborne.

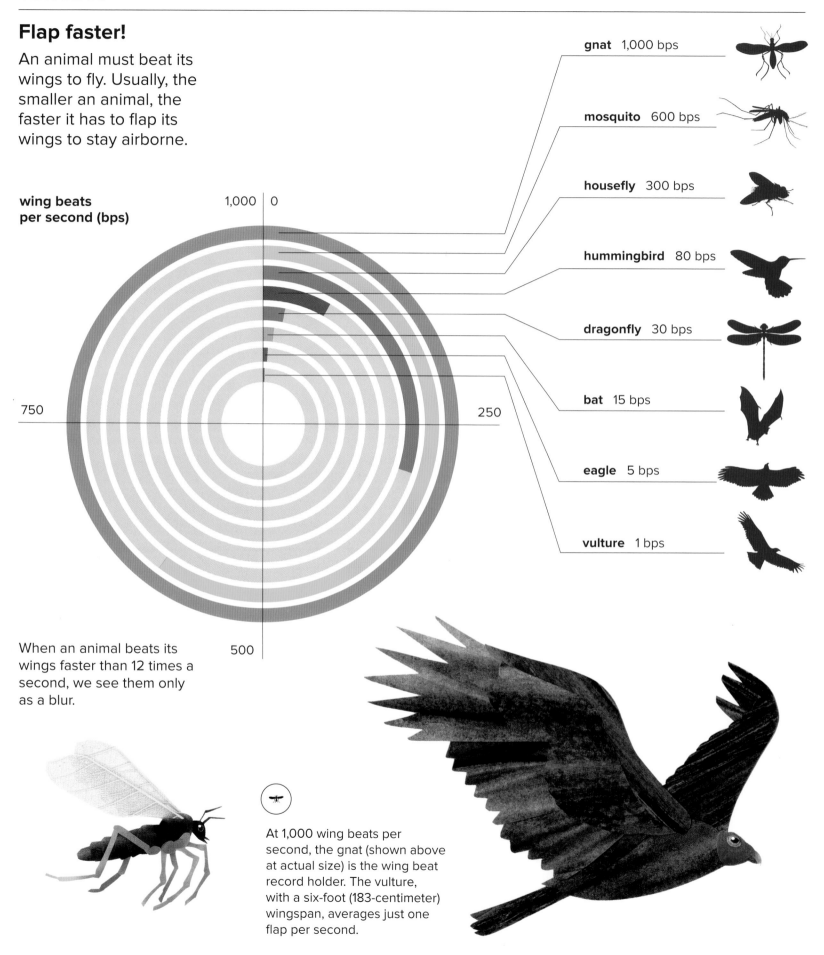

wing beats per second (bps)

1,000 0

750

250

500

gnat 1,000 bps

mosquito 600 bps

housefly 300 bps

hummingbird 80 bps

dragonfly 30 bps

bat 15 bps

eagle 5 bps

vulture 1 bps

When an animal beats its wings faster than 12 times a second, we see them only as a blur.

At 1,000 wing beats per second, the gnat (shown above at actual size) is the wing beat record holder. The vulture, with a six-foot (183-centimeter) wingspan, averages just one flap per second.

Sweet dreams

Most animals sleep, or seem to. It's difficult to tell if a worm or other simple animal is sleeping, but we do know that all mammals and most reptiles sleep, and possibly dream.

Giraffes, horses, and many other grazing animals often sleep standing up. This helps them escape or defend themselves if danger threatens. Bats sleep upside down, a position that allows them to take flight by simply letting go.

 hours awake

hours asleep

How many hours in a 24-hour day do animals sleep?

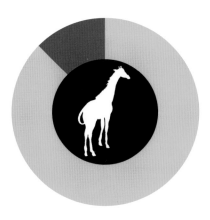

giraffe 2½ hours of sleep

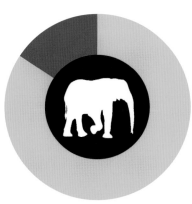

elephant 3½ hours of sleep

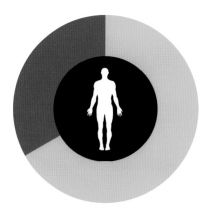

human 8 hours of sleep

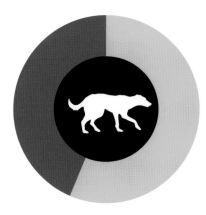

dog 10½ hours of sleep

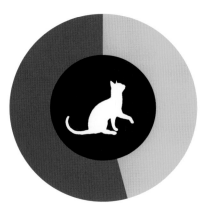

cat 13 hours of sleep

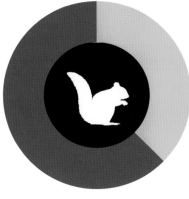

squirrel 15 hours of sleep

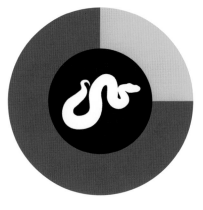

python 18 hours of sleep

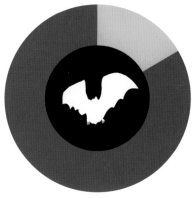

brown bat 20 hours of sleep

Long and short

The lives of some animals are over in a day or less. Other creatures can survive for hundreds of years.

This 507-year-old **quahog clam** holds the animal life span record. We don't know how long it might have lived. Scientists, planning to study it later, froze it before they realized how ancient it was.

- insects and spiders
- fish
- reptiles and amphibians
- birds
- mammals
- other invertebrates

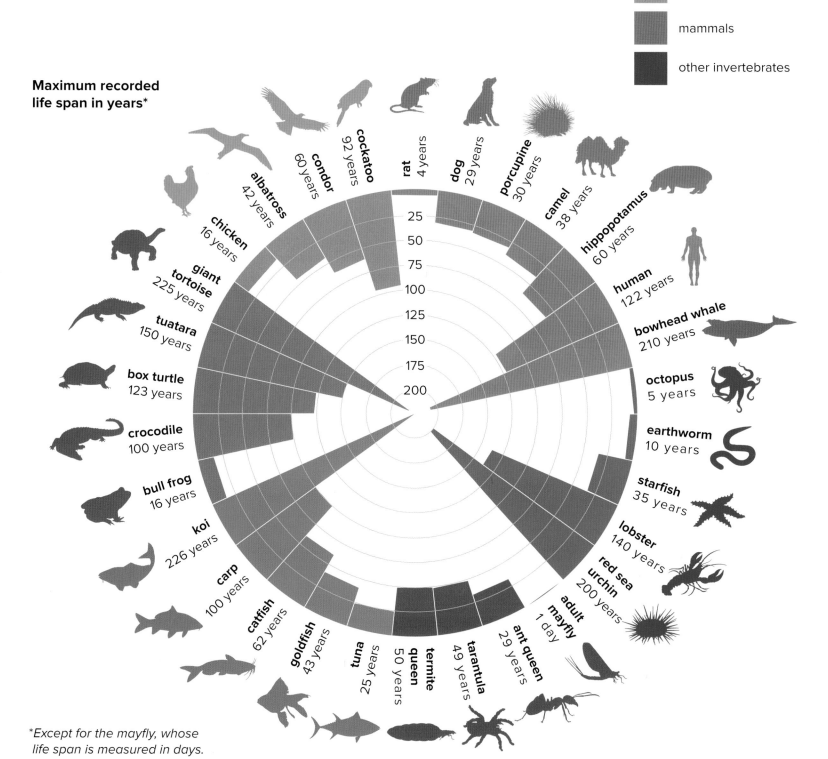

Maximum recorded life span in years*

cockatoo 92 years
rat 4 years
dog 29 years
porcupine 30 years
camel 38 years
hippopotamus 60 years
human 122 years
bowhead whale 210 years
octopus 5 years
earthworm 10 years
starfish 35 years
lobster 140 years
red sea urchin 200 years
adult mayfly 1 day
ant queen 29 years
tarantula 49 years
termite queen 50 years
tuna 25 years
goldfish 43 years
catfish 62 years
carp 100 years
koi 226 years
bull frog 16 years
crocodile 100 years
box turtle 123 years
tuatara 150 years
giant tortoise 225 years
chicken 16 years
albatross 42 years
condor 60 years

25
50
75
100
125
150
175
200

*Except for the mayfly, whose life span is measured in days.

22

Flutter or thump?

The heart rate of a warm-blooded animal is related to its body size. Large animals usually have slower heart rates than small animals.

An adult human hand compared to a hummingbird heart and a human heart.

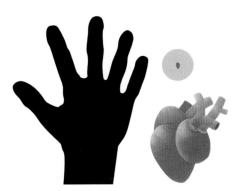

The heart of a blue whale is shown at the same scale as the two children.

Heartbeats per minute and body weight

hummingbird	shrew	mouse	chicken	rabbit	cat	human	horse	elephant	blue whale
1,200 bpm	800 bpm	650 bpm	275 bpm	200 bpm	130 bpm	70 bpm	35 bpm	30 bpm	10 bpm
⅒ ounce (3 gms)	⅓ ounce (9 gms)	¾ ounce (21 gms)	4 pounds (1¾ kgs)	7 pounds (3 kgs)	10 pounds (4½ kgs)	140 pounds (64 kgs)	1,000 pounds (454 kgs)	12,000 pounds (5,443 kgs)	200 tons (181,000 kgs)

♥ each heart = 10 beats per minute (bpm)

weight abbreviations:
gms = grams
kgs = kilograms

23

Serious headgear

Animals with horns are typically the males of their species. If the females have horns, they are usually smaller. This may be because males often use their horns in battles with other males over mates or territory.

The male **greater kudu** has some of the longest horns in the animal kingdom.

six feet
(183 centimeters)

five feet
(152 centimeters)

four feet
(122 centimeters)

three feet
(91 centimeters)

two feet
(61 centimeters)

one foot
(30 centimeters)

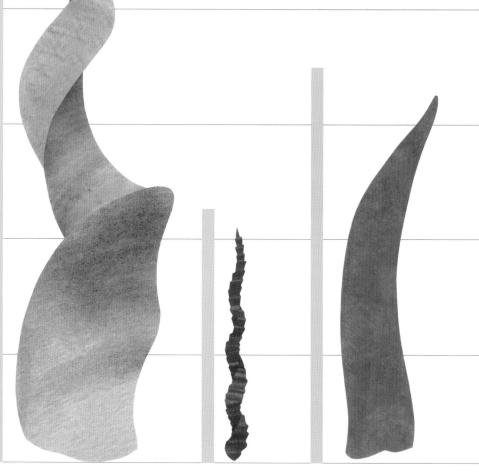

Deer and elk have antlers rather than horns. Antlers are made of bone and are shed and regrown every year. Horns are permanent and continue to grow throughout an animal's life.

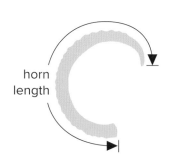

horn length

As shown above, horn length is measured along the curve of the horn. The bars represent horn lengths measured this way.

markhor
64 inches
(163 centimeters)

blackbuck
27 inches
(69 centimeters)

Watusi bull
42 inches
(107 centimeters)

The horns of the **Jackson's chameleon** and the **white rhinoceros,** like those of other horned animals, are made of bone covered in keratin—the same substance that forms your hair and fingernails.

greater kudu
6 feet
(183 centimeters)

white rhinoceros
5 feet
(152 centimeters)

Jackson's chameleon
1 inch
(2½ centimeters)

ibex
39 inches
(1 meter)

scimitar-horned oryx
4 feet
(122 centimeters)

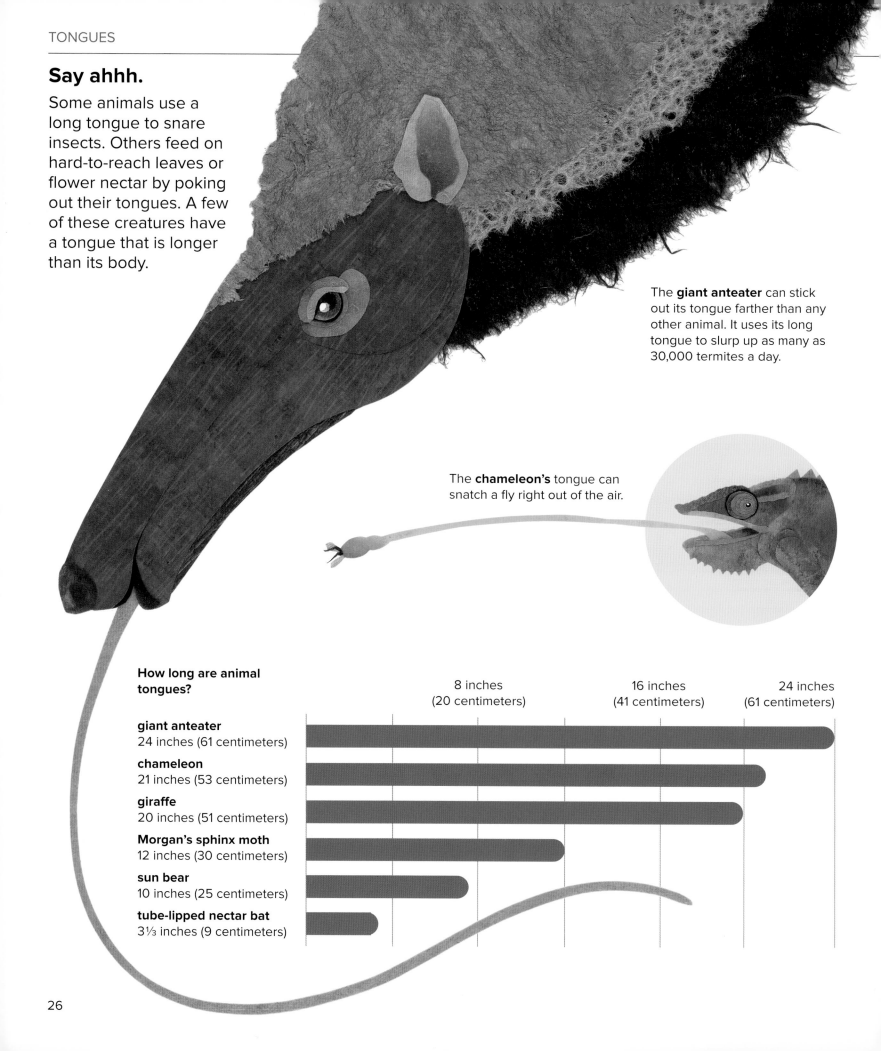

Say ahhh.

Some animals use a long tongue to snare insects. Others feed on hard-to-reach leaves or flower nectar by poking out their tongues. A few of these creatures have a tongue that is longer than its body.

The **giant anteater** can stick out its tongue farther than any other animal. It uses its long tongue to slurp up as many as 30,000 termites a day.

The **chameleon's** tongue can snatch a fly right out of the air.

How long are animal tongues?

	8 inches (20 centimeters)	16 inches (41 centimeters)	24 inches (61 centimeters)

giant anteater
24 inches (61 centimeters)

chameleon
21 inches (53 centimeters)

giraffe
20 inches (51 centimeters)

Morgan's sphinx moth
12 inches (30 centimeters)

sun bear
10 inches (25 centimeters)

tube-lipped nectar bat
3⅓ inches (9 centimeters)

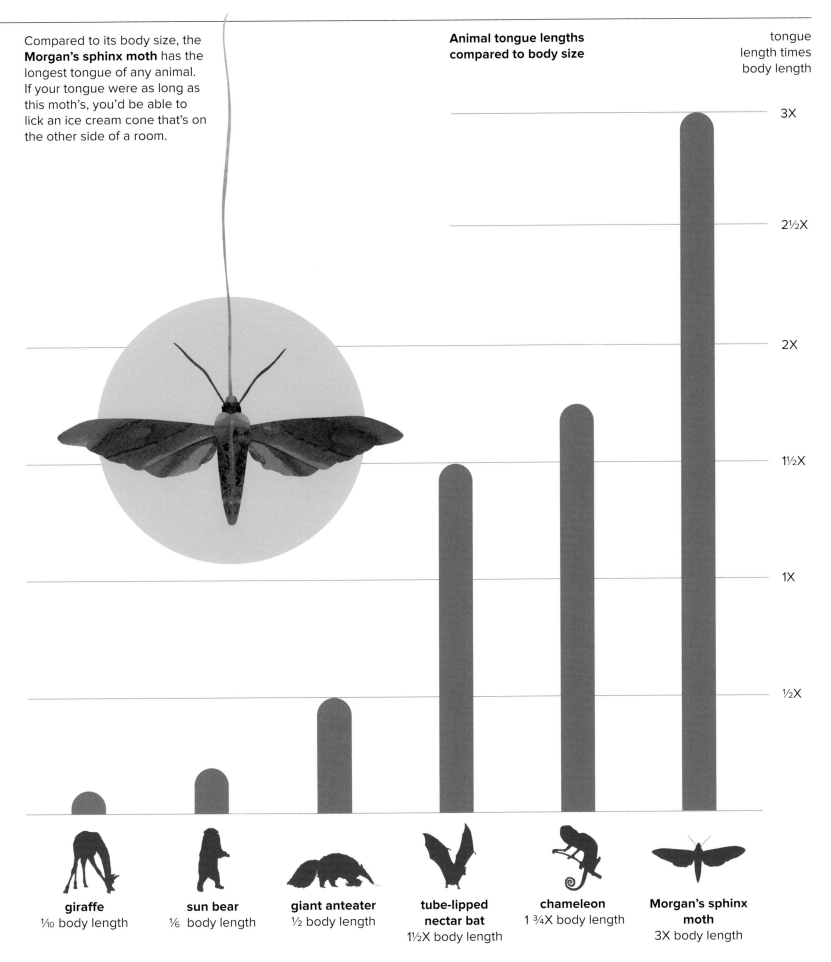

Compared to its body size, the **Morgan's sphinx moth** has the longest tongue of any animal. If your tongue were as long as this moth's, you'd be able to lick an ice cream cone that's on the other side of a room.

Animal tongue lengths compared to body size

tongue length times body length

3X

2½X

2X

1½X

1X

½X

giraffe
1/10 body length

sun bear
1/6 body length

giant anteater
½ body length

tube-lipped nectar bat
1½X body length

chameleon
1 ¾X body length

Morgan's sphinx moth
3X body length

Loud and louder

Animals use squawks, roars, chirps, and clicks to communicate, to defend their territory, even as a weapon to kill their prey. Many animals can produce sounds that are painfully loud to us.

Elephants communicate by making a deep rumbling sound that carries for miles. It's loud, but it's pitched too low for human ears to hear.

The **bush cricket** makes a sound as loud as a chainsaw by rubbing its legs together.

A chainsaw is this loud

wolf
115 decibels

elephant
115 decibels

bush cricket
110 decibels

hyena
110 decibels

lion
110 decibels

macaw
105 decibels

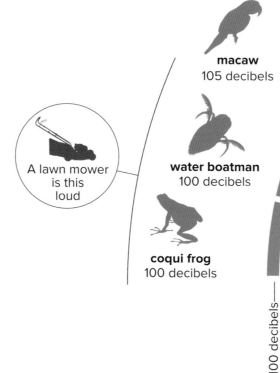

A lawn mower is this loud

water boatman
100 decibels

coqui frog
100 decibels

What is a decibel?
Scientists measure sound with units called *decibels*. Zero decibels is the quietest sound that a human can detect. Sixty decibels is the level of normal conversation. Above 120 decibels, sounds are painful and damaging to human ears.

▬▬▬▬ decibels in air

▬▬▬▬ decibels in water

Sound is measured differently in water and in air. The darker bars allow us to compare an underwater sound to one measured in the air.

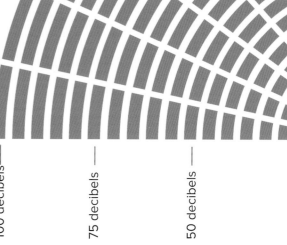

100 decibels   75 decibels   50 decibels

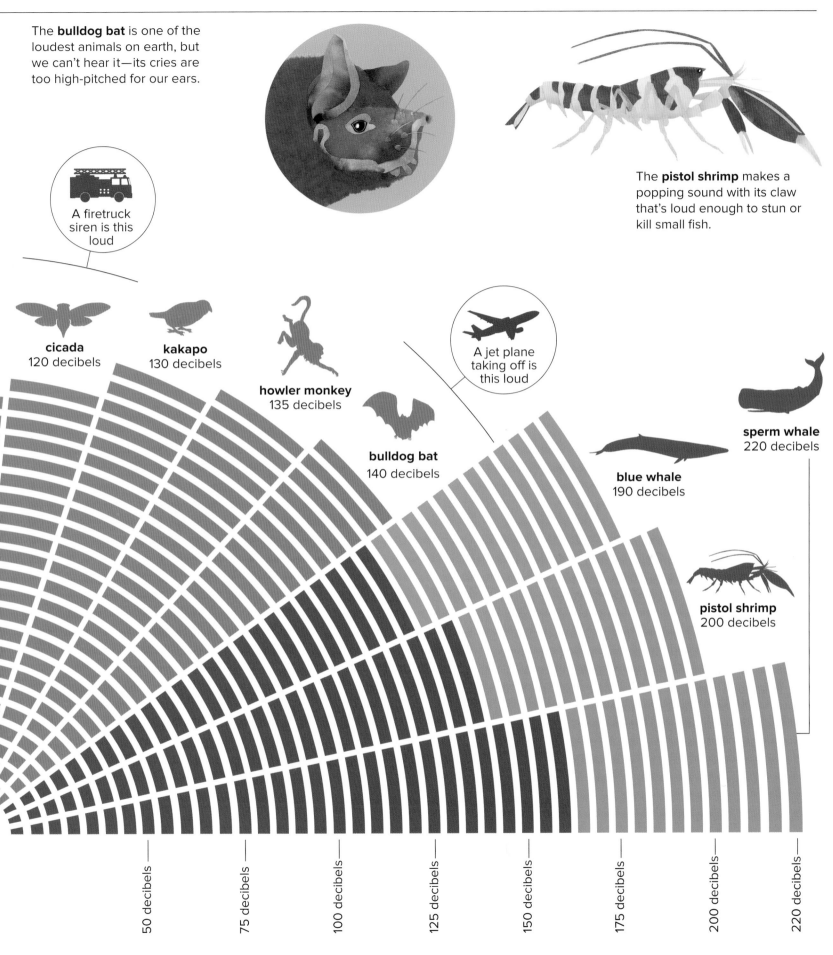

The **bulldog bat** is one of the loudest animals on earth, but we can't hear it—its cries are too high-pitched for our ears.

The **pistol shrimp** makes a popping sound with its claw that's loud enough to stun or kill small fish.

A firetruck siren is this loud

A jet plane taking off is this loud

cicada
120 decibels

kakapo
130 decibels

howler monkey
135 decibels

bulldog bat
140 decibels

blue whale
190 decibels

sperm whale
220 decibels

pistol shrimp
200 decibels

50 decibels

75 decibels

100 decibels

125 decibels

150 decibels

175 decibels

200 decibels

220 decibels

Decisions, decisions.

When a three-banded armadillo realizes that another animal is approaching, it must make quick decisions about how to stay safe.

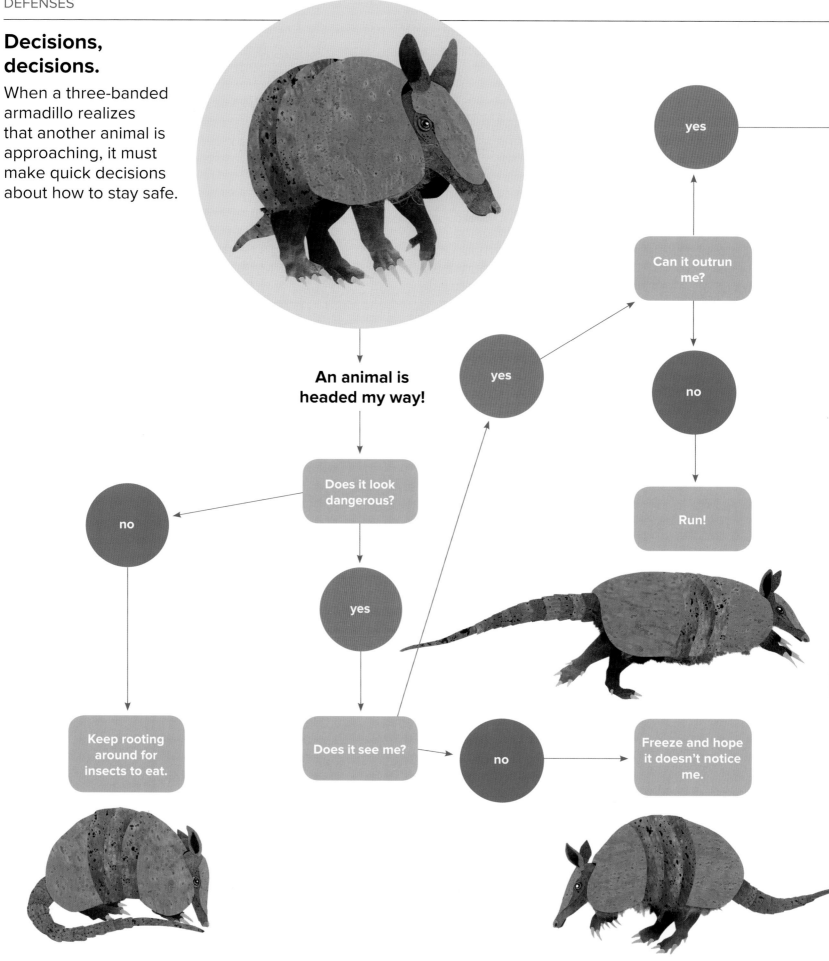

An animal is headed my way!

Does it look dangerous?

no

yes

Keep rooting around for insects to eat.

Does it see me?

no

Freeze and hope it doesn't notice me.

yes

Can it outrun me?

yes

no

Run!

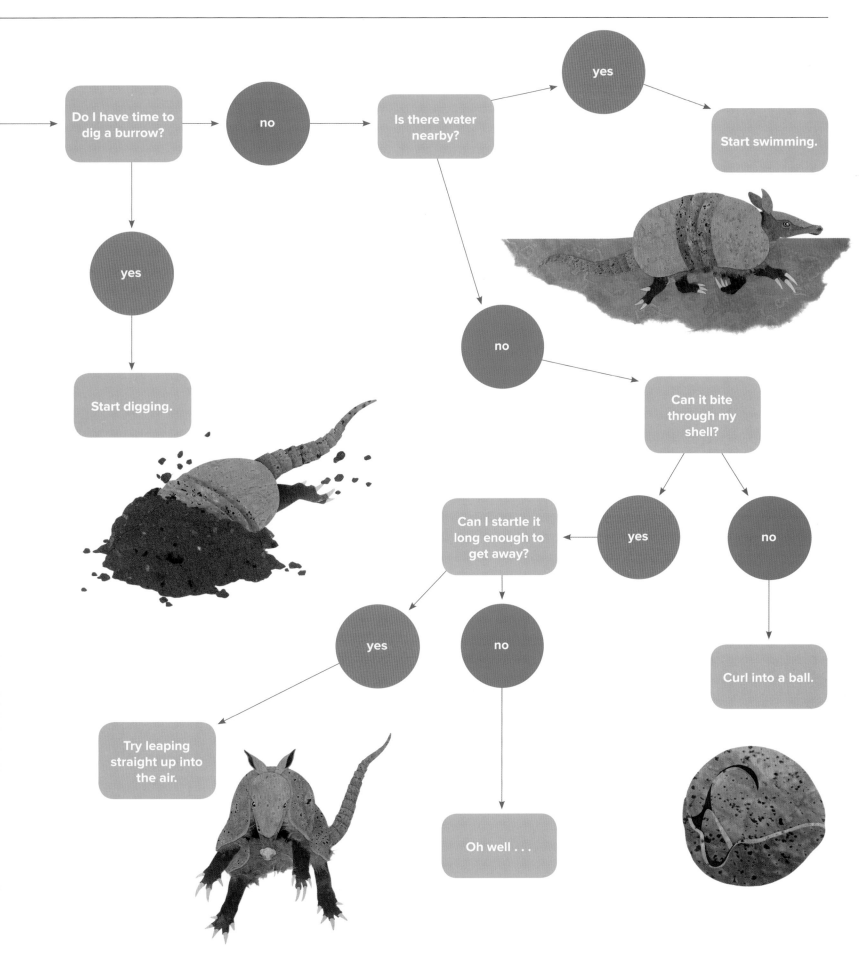

Do I have time to dig a burrow?

no → Is there water nearby?

yes → Start swimming.

yes → Start digging.

no → Can it bite through my shell?

yes → Can I startle it long enough to get away?

no → Curl into a ball.

yes → Try leaping straight up into the air.

no → Oh well . . .

Deadly

Many animals use poison or venom to kill their prey or defend themselves. *Poisonous* animals have toxins in their flesh or skin. They must be touched or eaten to cause harm. *Venomous* animals inject toxins with stings, teeth, or spines.

golden poison dart frog
The toxins in this frog's skin are the most powerful of any animal.

beadlet anemone
The tentacles of this flower-like creature contain the second most toxic venom in the animal kingdom.

inland taipan
Its fangs deliver the most potent venom of any snake.

marbled cone shell
This shellfish hunts by firing a venomous dart into its prey.

box jellyfish
This tiny creature's venom kills more people than any other animal on this page.

Sydney funnel-web spider
The world's most venomous spider lives in Australia.

 poisonous
(toxic skin or flesh)

 venomous
(injects venom)

 poisonous skin
or flesh
(toxic skin or body)

 venomous barbs,
spines, or stinging
cells

 venomous teeth
or fangs

reef stonefish
Its thirteen spines can inject the most deadly venom of any fish.

puffer fish
This fish is dangerous only if eaten—its skin and some of its internal organs are poisonous. Its toxins would be stronger if injected—when eaten, they lose some of their potency.

blue-ringed octopus
Its venom may not be as powerful as that of the other animals pictured, but don't underestimate it: a bite from this little octopus can kill a person within minutes.

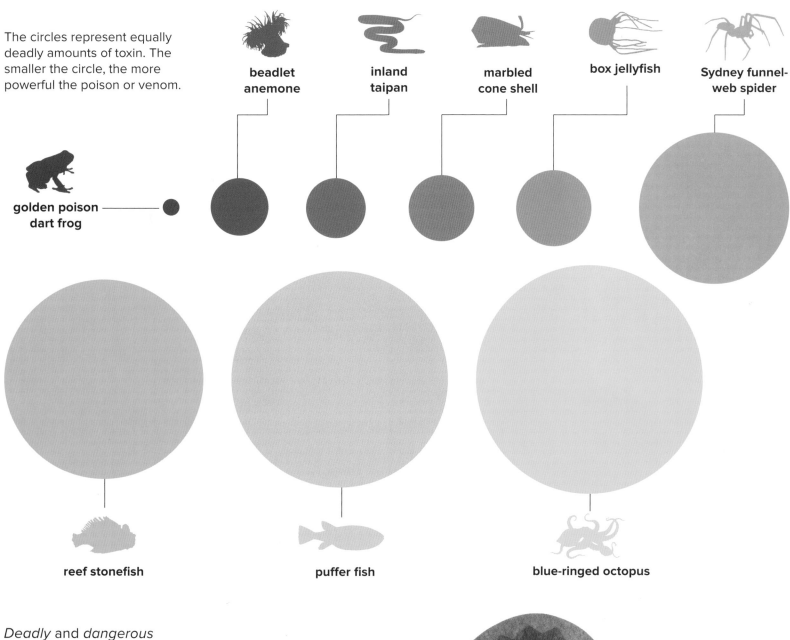

The circles represent equally deadly amounts of toxin. The smaller the circle, the more powerful the poison or venom.

beadlet anemone

inland taipan

marbled cone shell

box jellyfish

Sydney funnel-web spider

golden poison dart frog

reef stonefish

puffer fish

blue-ringed octopus

Deadly and dangerous aren't always the same thing. The **beadlet anemone,** for example, has powerful venom but causes few if any human deaths. Other animals with less potent toxins can be more dangerous. They might be especially aggressive or deliver more venom with a bite or sting. The **Russel's viper** is not as venomous as some other creatures, but an estimated 25,000 people die from its bite every year.

Which animals cause the most human deaths?

In many parts of the world, animals are a serious threat to humans. Some see people as prey. Others use venom to hunt or defend themselves. Even more dangerous are animals that carry deadly diseases.

The **hippopotamus** appears to be a peaceful animal. But it will react aggressively if it feels threatened, making it one of the world's most dangerous large animals.

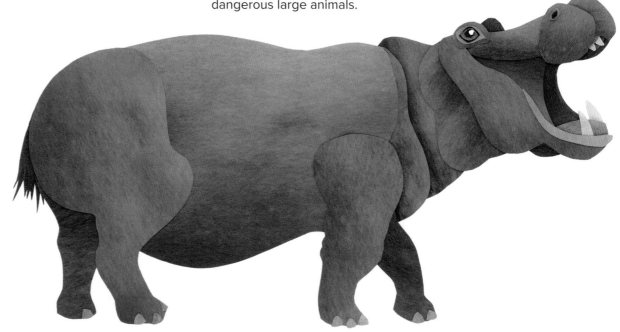

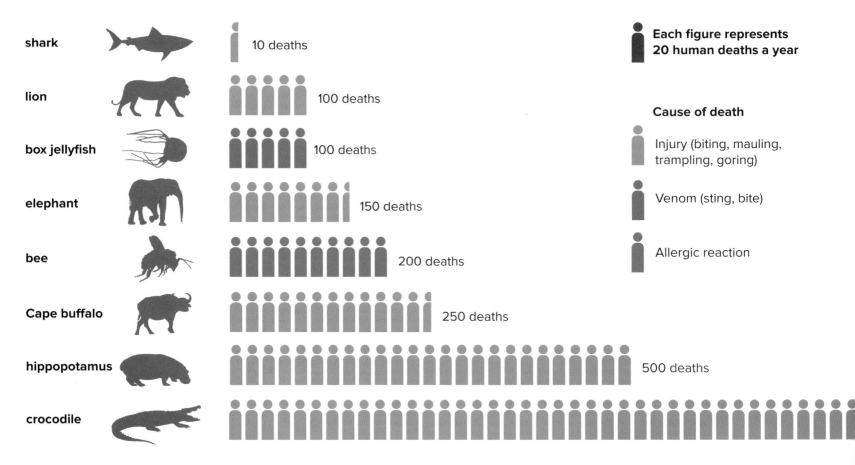

shark — 10 deaths

lion — 100 deaths

box jellyfish — 100 deaths

elephant — 150 deaths

bee — 200 deaths

Cape buffalo — 250 deaths

hippopotamus — 500 deaths

crocodile

Each figure represents 20 human deaths a year

Cause of death

Injury (biting, mauling, trampling, goring)

Venom (sting, bite)

Allergic reaction

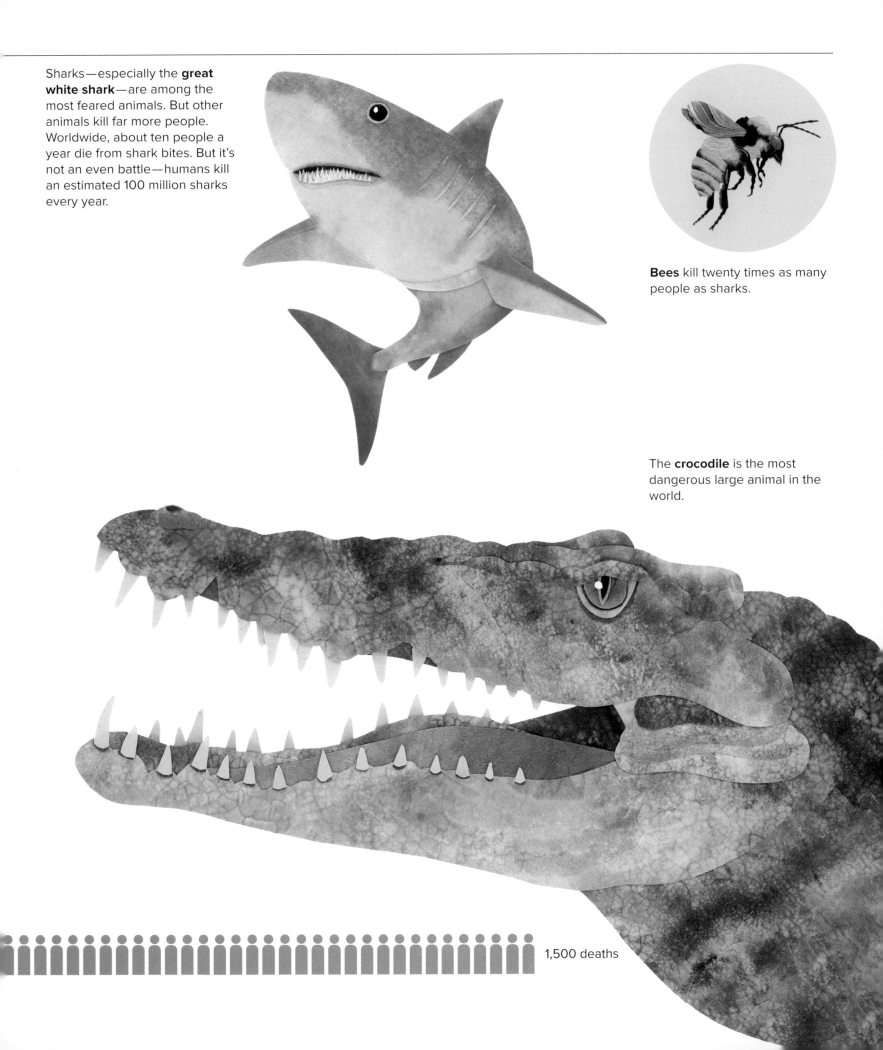

Sharks—especially the **great white shark**—are among the most feared animals. But other animals kill far more people. Worldwide, about ten people a year die from shark bites. But it's not an even battle—humans kill an estimated 100 million sharks every year.

Bees kill twenty times as many people as sharks.

The **crocodile** is the most dangerous large animal in the world.

1,500 deaths

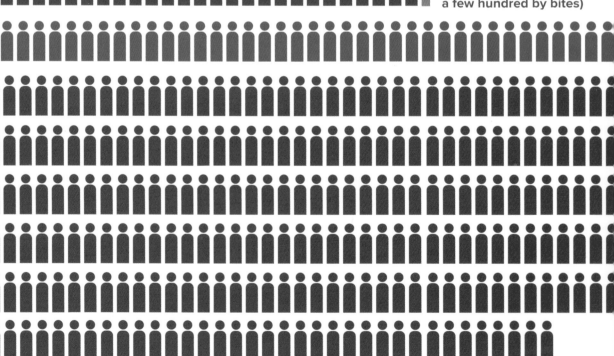

It's not surprising that highly venomous animals, such as the **fat-tailed scorpion** and the **krait,** are deadly. But most people don't realize how dangerous **dogs** are. Even a minor dog bite can transmit rabies, a deadly disease. The **tsetse fly** is also a deadly disease carrier.

fat-tailed scorpion

krait

tsetse fly

fat-tailed scorpion 5,000 deaths

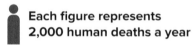 Each figure represents **2,000 human deaths a year**

tsetse fly 10,000 deaths (carries sleeping sickness)

dog  55,000 deaths (most by rabies, a few hundred by bites)

snake

mosquito

Cause of death

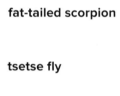 Injury (biting, mauling, trampling, goring)

 Venom (sting, bite)

Disease (spread by bite)

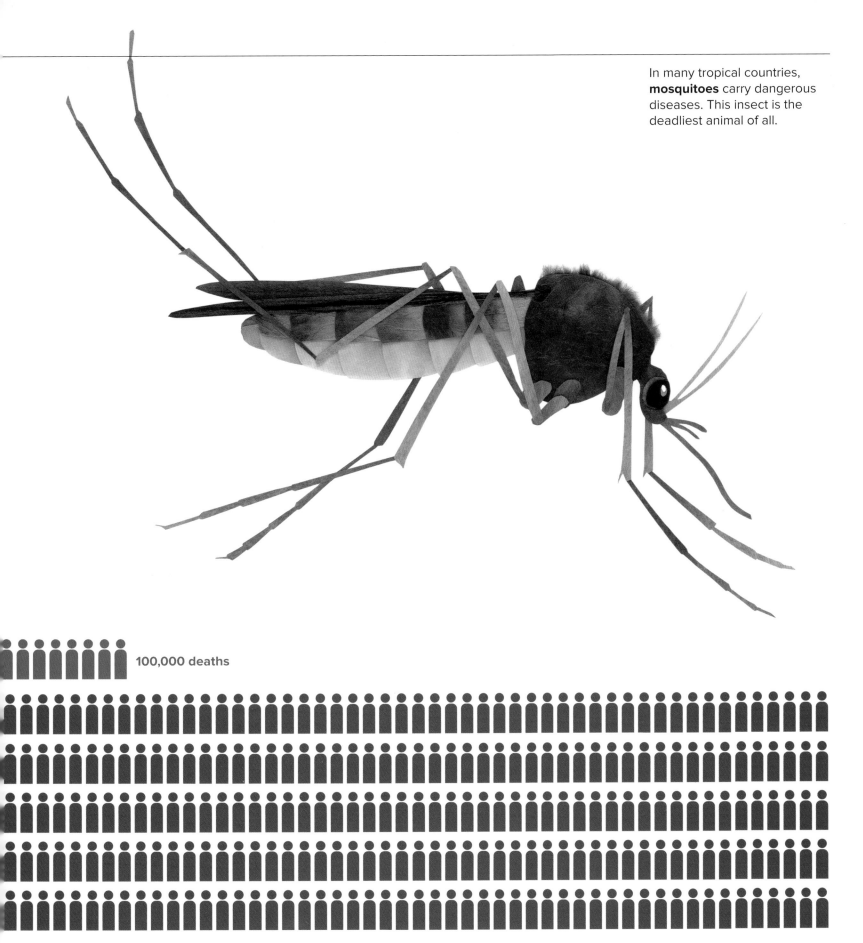

In many tropical countries, **mosquitoes** carry dangerous diseases. This insect is the deadliest animal of all.

100,000 deaths

1,000,000 deaths (transmits malaria and other diseases)

High and low

At high altitude, it's difficult for animals to get enough oxygen. But surviving deep in the sea presents other challenges. The water pressure—the weight of all the water above— would crush any creature not specially adapted to live there.

40,000 feet
(12,192 meters)

Rüpell's vulture
(highest bird flight)
37,000 feet
(11,278 meters)

The summit of Mount Everest, the highest point on earth. Here the atmospheric pressure is just 1/3 that at sea level.

29,029 feet (8,848 meters).

30,000 feet
(9,144 meters)

blue sheep
20,000 feet
(6,096 meters)

Himalayan jumping spider
(highest permanent animal habitat)
22,000 feet
(6,705 meters)

20,000 feet
(6,096 meters)

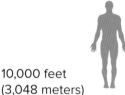

La Rinoconada, Peru
(highest permanent human settlement)
16,700 feet
(5,090 meters)

Himalayan viper
(highest reptile)
16,000 feet
(4,877 meters)

10,000 feet
(3,048 meters)

Mexican free-tailed bat
10,000 feet
(3,048 meters)

sea level

thick-billed murre
690 feet
(210 meters)

human diver
(deepest dive without equipment)
702 feet
(214 meters)

beaked whale
(deepest mammal dive)
9,800 feet
(2,987 meters)

10,000 feet
(3,048 meters)

20,000 feet
(6,096 meters)

snailfish
(deepest fish)
26,722 feet
(8,145 meters)

30,000 feet
(9,144 meters)

The Mariana Trench is the deepest spot in the sea. Here the pressure is more than 1,000 times greater than at sea level.

36,070 feet (10,994 meters)

supergiant amphipod
36,070 feet
(10,994 meters)

above
sea level

below
sea level

The **Himalayan jumping spider** lives four miles (6½ kilometers) above sea level.

In 1973 a jet plane collided with a **Rüpell's vulture** at 37,000 feet (11,278 meters)—an altitude record for bird flight. The plane was unharmed, but the vulture did not fare as well.

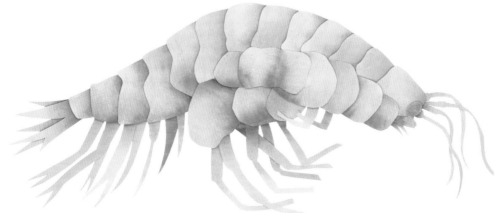

For a long time, scientists believed that no animal could survive the enormous pressures in the deepest parts of the sea. When they finally reached the bottom of the Mariana Trench, they were surprised to find a **supergiant amphipod**—a shrimplike creature almost a foot (30 centimeters) long.

Hot and cold

A few animals thrive in some of the most extreme temperatures on earth. These creatures are adapted to live in habitats so hot or so cold that most other animals would quickly perish.

The body of the **Pompeii worm** is covered in heat-loving bacteria that produce its food. The worm places its tail in hot water streaming from undersea volcanic vents but keeps its head in cooler water.

The **emporer penguin** spends the Anarctic winter standing in the open. It endures some of the coldest temperatures on earth.

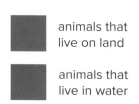

■ animals that live on land

■ animals that live in water

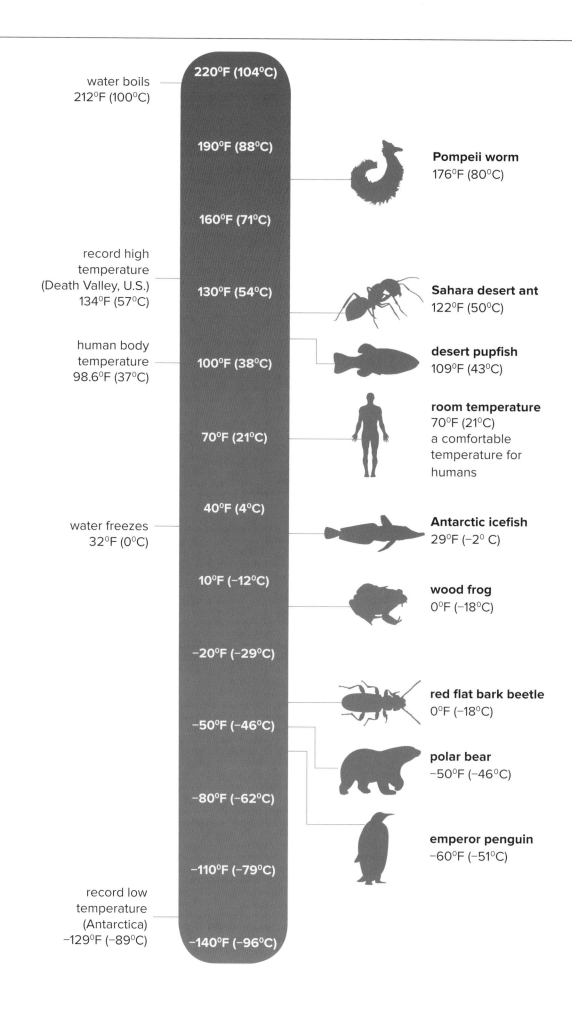

water boils
212°F (100°C)

220°F (104°C)

190°F (88°C)

Pompeii worm
176°F (80°C)

160°F (71°C)

record high
temperature
(Death Valley, U.S.)
134°F (57°C)

130°F (54°C)

Sahara desert ant
122°F (50°C)

human body
temperature
98.6°F (37°C)

100°F (38°C)

desert pupfish
109°F (43°C)

room temperature
70°F (21°C)
a comfortable
temperature for
humans

70°F (21°C)

40°F (4°C)

water freezes
32°F (0°C)

Antarctic icefish
29°F (−2° C)

10°F (−12°C)

wood frog
0°F (−18°C)

−20°F (−29°C)

−50°F (−46°C)

red flat bark beetle
0°F (−18°C)

polar bear
−50°F (−46°C)

−80°F (−62°C)

emperor penguin
−60°F (−51°C)

−110°F (−79°C)

record low
temperature
(Antarctica)
−129°F (−89°C)

−140°F (−96°C)

The tiny **tardigrade,** or **water bear,** lives almost everywhere on earth. It is by far the hot and cold champion of the animal world. By dehydrating itself—eliminating water from its body—it can survive conditions as cold as −328°F (−200°C) and as hot as 304°F (151°C). Tardigrades have even survived for days in the cold and vacuum of space.

In the circle is a **tardigrade** shown life size.

World travelers

Some animals travel
a long way to find
food, mates, or a new
place to live. When this
happens on a regular
schedule—often timed
with a change of season
—it is called *migration*.

The **arctic tern** flies from the
far north to Antarctica and back
every year. It travels farther
than any other animal in its
annual migration.

Annual migration distance

	5,000 miles (8,047 kilometers)	10,000 miles (16,093 kilometers)	15,000 miles (24,140 kilometers)

wildebeest — 1,000 miles (1,609 kilometers)

Brent goose — 3,700 miles (5,955 kilometers)

monarch butterfly — 5,000 miles (8,047 kilometers)

leatherback sea turtle — 7,400 miles (11,909 kilometers)

globe skimmer dragonfly — 11,000 miles (17,703 kilometers)

gray whale — 12,000 miles (19,312 kilometers)

great white shark — 12,400 miles (19,956 kilometers)

sooty shearwater

arctic tern

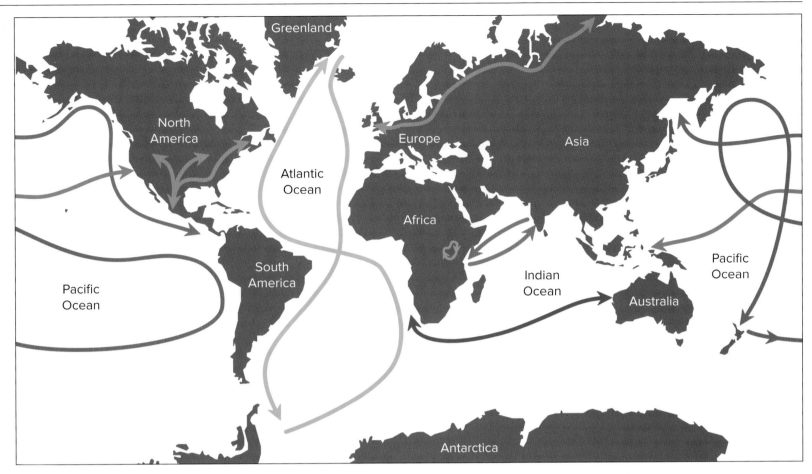

wildebeest

Brent goose

monarch butterfly

leatherback sea turtle

globe skimmer dragonfly

gray whale

great white shark

sooty shearwater

arctic tern

Evey year more than a million **wildebeests** take part in the largest migration of land animals on earth.

| 25,000 miles (40,234 kilometers) | 30,000 miles (48,280 kilometers) | 35,000 miles (56,327 kilometers) | 40,000 miles (64,374 kilometers) | 45,000 miles (72,420 kilometers) |

40,000 miles (64,374 kilometers)

44,000 miles (70,811 kilometers)

Disaster!

Earth has experienced at least five mass extinctions within the past 500 million years. Each of these events caused more than half of the animal species alive at the time to become extinct. But these disasters also produced some winners: animals who were able to thrive once their competitors were gone.

Dinosaurs are probably the most famous extinct animals. But they are not alone—more than 99 percent of all the animals that have ever lived are now extinct. Many of them died out in one of the five great mass extinctions.

In each mass extinction, many kinds of animals die off, leaving the field clear for other, luckier creatures. The graphs show only a few of the most well known.

 percent of species that became extinct

 percent of species that survived

Possible causes of extinction

 climate change

 volcanic activity

 asteroid or comet impact

 human activity

500 million years ago | 450 million years ago | 400 million years ago | 350 million years ago

440 million years ago

85%
of animal species died

losers:
nautiloids, corals, shellfish

winners: crinoids
(plantlike animals)

The earth was colder, and glaciers locked up much of the world's water. No animals lived on land.

360 million years ago

75%
of animal species died

losers:
armored fish, corals

**winners:
sharks and bony fish**

This event lasted around 20 million years. It could have been the result of drastic climate and sea level changes.

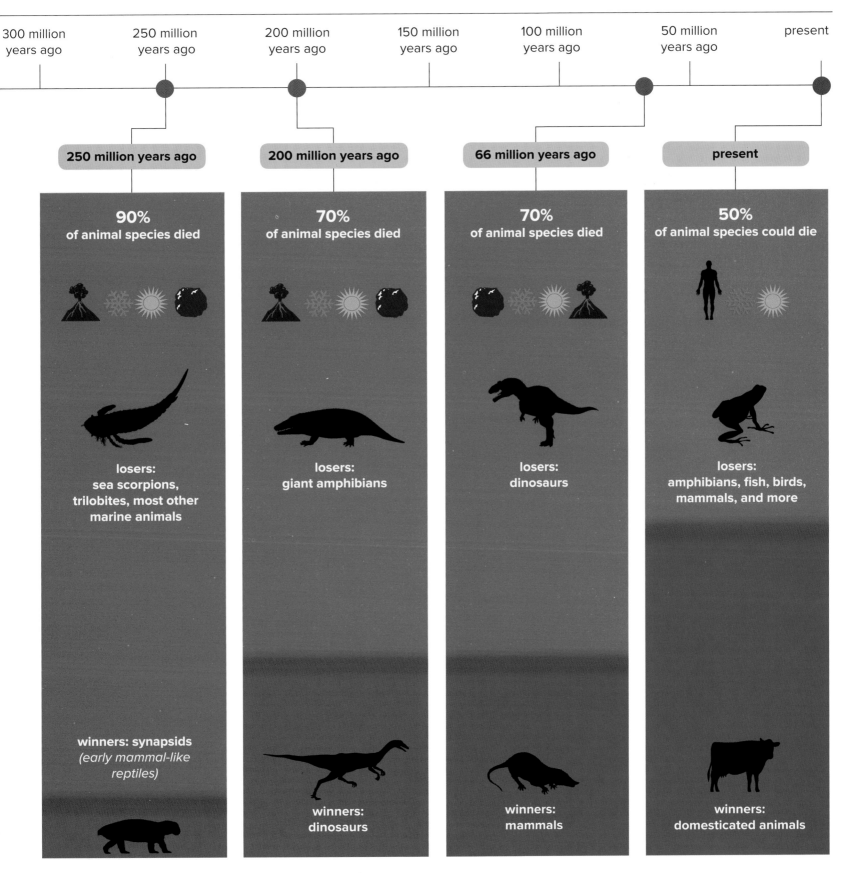

| 300 million years ago | 250 million years ago | 200 million years ago | 150 million years ago | 100 million years ago | 50 million years ago | present |

250 million years ago

90%
of animal species died

losers:
sea scorpions,
trilobites, most other
marine animals

winners: synapsids
*(early mammal-like
reptiles)*

The greatest of all mass
extinctions. It may have been
caused by an asteroid or comet
impact, volcanic activity, or both.

200 million years ago

70%
of animal species died

losers:
giant amphibians

winners:
dinosaurs

Volcanic activity might be the
main cause of this extinction.

66 million years ago

70%
of animal species died

losers:
dinosaurs

winners:
mammals

A city-size asteroid crashed
into the earth, causing terrible
destruction. Massive lava flows
probably contributed.

present

50%
of animal species could die

losers:
amphibians, fish, birds,
mammals, and more

winners:
domesticated animals

We are in the midst of a sixth
mass extinction caused by
humans. In the next 50 years, half
of all animal species could die.

Almost gone

These animals are among the most endangered on earth. There are fewer than 100 of any of these creatures still alive.

The **Red River giant soft-shelled turtle** is perhaps the world's most endangered animal. As far as we know, there are just three of these turtles still alive. Two are in zoos, and one is in a lake in Vietnam.

 = one animal

What is threatening them?

 habitat loss

 collecting

 hunting/poaching

 fishing/poaching

	Miami blue butterfly fewer than 100 left		
	Golden-headed langur 70 left		
	Javan rhino 60 left		
	Spix macaw 40 left		
	Amur leopard 35 left		
	Bajii dolphin 20 left (?)		
	Red River soft-shelled turtle 3 left		

46

The **bajii** is a freshwater dolphin native to China's Yangtze River. It's population of 20 is a guess—it may already be extinct.

The world's most endangered primate is the **golden-headed langur.** It is hunted for food and its forest home is being cut down.

In 1992, a hurricane destroyed the only known colony of the **Miami blue butterfly**. A few years later, another small colony of these rare insects was discovered in Florida.

Poachers kill the **Javan rhinoceros** because they mistakenly believe its horn has magical properties.

The **Amur leopard** is the world's most endangered large cat. It has been hunted almost to extinction for its fur.

A few years ago, only 17 **Spix macaws** were alive. Since then, birds bred in captivity have begun to increase their numbers.

The facts and figures in this book come from many different sources. Some are included in the bibliography below, but there are too many to list all of them.

Much of the data in the book is well documented. It's not that difficult to find out how big an animal is, to measure the length of its horns, or to count its wing beats. Other facts are the educated guesses of scientists—we don't know exactly how much all the squid in the oceans weigh, or how long a clam can live. In many cases, such as the speed of a peregrine falcon or the number of mollusk species, there are a wide range of figures given by credible sources. In those cases, I've consulted many sources and generally used numbers from the middle of the range.

Bibliography

Books:

Amazing Biofacts. By Susan Goodman. Peter Bedrick Books, 1993.

Amazing Numbers in Biology. By Rainer Flindt. Springer-Verlag, 2006.

Animal Records. By Mark Carwardine. Sterling Publishing, 2008.

The Book of Life. Edited by Stephen J. Gould. W. W. Norton & Company, 1993.

Fantastic Book of Comparisons. By Russell Ash. Dorling Kindersley, 1997.

The Infographic History of the World. By Valentina D'Efilippo & James Ball. Firefly Books, 2014.

Information Everywhere. Edited by Jenny Finch. Dorling Kindersley, 2010.

Knowledge Is Beautiful. By David McCandless. Harper Design, 2014.

National Geographic Animal Encyclopedia. By Jinny Johnson. Marshall Editions, 1999.

Venom: Poisonous Animals in the Natural World. By Steve Backshall. New Holland Publishers, 2007.

The Way Nature Works. Edited by Robin Rees. Macmillan, 1992.

Websites:

www.amnh.org (the American Museum of Natural History)

www.bbc.com/earth/uk (the BBC's natural history website)

www.iucnredlist.org (endangered animals)

www.nationalgeographic.com

www.si.edu (the Smithsonian Institution)

ISBN 978-0-544-63092-5

Manufactured in China
SCP 10 9 8 7 6 5 4 3 2 1
4500602147